LEPTIN RESET

MEGA BUNDLE – 4 Manuscripts in 1 – 160+ Leptin Reset - friendly recipes including pie, cookie, and smoothies for a delicious and tasty diet

TABLE OF CONTENTS

publisher. All rights reserved.

Introduction

Leptin Reset recipes for personal enjoyment but also for family enjoyment. You will love them for sure for how easy it is to prepare them.

BEANS OMELETTE

Serves: **1**
Prep Time: **5**   Minutes

Cook Time: **10** Minutes

Total Time: **15** Minutes

INGREDIENTS

- 2 eggs
- ¼ tsp salt
- ¼ tsp black pepper
- 1 tablespoon olive oil
- ¼ cup cheese
- ¼ tsp basil
- 1 cup beans

DIRECTIONS

1. In a bowl combine all ingredients together and mix well
2. In a skillet heat olive oil and pour the egg mixture
3. Cook for 1-2 minutes per side
4. When ready remove omelette from the skillet and serve

CORN OMELETTE

Serves: *1*

Prep Time: 5   Minutes

Cook Time: *10*   Minutes

Total Time: *15*   Minutes

INGREDIENTS

- 2 eggs
- ¼ cup cheese
- ¼ tsp basil
- 1 cup corn

DIRECTIONS

1. In a bowl combine all ingredients together and mix well
2. In a skillet heat olive oil and pour the egg mixture
3. Cook for 1-2 minutes per side
4. When ready remove omelette from the skillet and serve

BREAKFAST GRANOLA

Serves: 2

Prep Time: 5   Minutes

Cook Time: 30   Minutes

Total Time: 35   Minutes

INGREDIENTS

- 1 tsp vanilla extract
- 1 tablespoon honey
- 1 lb. rolled oats
- 2 tablespoons sesame seeds
- ¼ lb. almonds
- ¼ lb. berries

DIRECTIONS

1. Preheat the oven to 325 F
2. Spread the granola onto a baking sheet
3. Bake for 12-15 minutes, remove and mix everything
4. Bake for another 12-15 minutes or until slightly brown
5. When ready remove from the oven and serve

BLUEBERRY PANCAKES

Serves: **4**

Prep Time: **10**   Minutes

Cook Time: **20**   Minutes

Total Time: **30**   Minutes

INGREDIENTS

- 1 cup whole wheat flour
- ¼ tsp baking soda
- ¼ tsp baking powder
- 1 cup blueberries
- 2 eggs
- 1 cup milk

DIRECTIONS

1. In a bowl combine all ingredients together and mix well
2. In a skillet heat olive oil
3. Pour ¼ of the batter and cook each pancake for 1-2 minutes per side
4. When ready remove from heat and serve

MULBERRIES PANCAKES

Serves: **4**

Prep Time: **10**   Minutes

Cook Time: **30**   Minutes

Total Time: **40**   Minutes

INGREDIENTS

- 1 cup whole wheat flour
- ¼ tsp baking soda
- ¼ tsp baking powder
- 1 cup mulberries
- 2 eggs
- 1 cup milk

DIRECTIONS

1. In a bowl combine all ingredients together and mix well
2. In a skillet heat olive oil
3. Pour ¼ of the batter and cook each pancake for 1-2 minutes per side
4. When ready remove from heat and serve

BANANA PANCAKES

Serves: **4**

Prep Time: **10** Minutes

Cook Time: **20** Minutes

Total Time: **30** Minutes

INGREDIENTS

- 1 cup whole wheat flour
- ¼ tsp baking soda
- ¼ tsp baking powder
- 1 cup mashed banana
- 2 eggs
- 1 cup milk

DIRECTIONS

1. In a bowl combine all ingredients together and mix well
2. In a skillet heat olive oil
3. Pour ¼ of the batter and cook each pancake for 1-2 minutes per side
4. When ready remove from heat and serve

NECTARINE PANCAKES

Serves: *4*

Prep Time: *10*   Minutes

Cook Time: *20*   Minutes

Total Time: *30*   Minutes

INGREDIENTS

- 1 cup whole wheat flour
- ¼ tsp baking soda
- ¼ tsp baking powder
- 1 cup nectarines
- 2 eggs
- 1 cup milk

DIRECTIONS

1. In a bowl combine all ingredients together and mix well
2. In a skillet heat olive oil
3. Pour ¼ of the batter and cook each pancake for 1-2 minutes per side
4. When ready remove from heat and serve

PANCAKES

Serves: **4**

Prep Time: **10**   Minutes

Cook Time: **30**   Minutes

Total Time: **40**   Minutes

INGREDIENTS

- 1 cup whole wheat flour
- ¼ tsp baking soda
- ¼ tsp baking powder
- 2 eggs
- 1 cup milk

DIRECTIONS

1. In a bowl combine all ingredients together and mix well
2. In a skillet heat olive oil
3. Pour ¼ of the batter and cook each pancake for 1-2 minutes per side
4. When ready remove from heat and serve

Serves: *1*

Prep Time: 5   Minutes

Cook Time: 5   Minutes

Total Time: *10*   Minutes

INGREDIENTS

- ½ cup dried raisins
- ½ cup dried pecans
- ¼ cup almonds
- 1 cup coconut milk
- 1 tsp cinnamon

DIRECTIONS

1. In a bowl combine all ingredients together
2. Serve with milk

SAUSAGE BREAKFAST SANDWICH

Serves: **2**
Prep Time: **5**   Minutes

Cook Time: **15**   Minutes

Total Time: **20**   Minutes

INGREDIENTS

- ¼ cup egg substitute
- 1 muffin
- 1 turkey sausage patty
- 1 tablespoon cheddar cheese

DIRECTIONS

1. In a skillet pour egg and cook on low heat
2. Place turkey sausage patty in a pan and cook for 4-5 minutes per side
3. On a toasted muffin place the cooked egg, top with a sausage patty and cheddar cheese
4. Serve when ready

LEMON MUFFINS

Serves: *8-12*

Prep Time: *10*   Minutes

Cook Time: *20*   Minutes

Total Time: *30*   Minutes

INGREDIENTS

- 2 eggs
- 1 tablespoon olive oil
- 1 cup milk
- 2 cups whole wheat flour
- 1 tsp baking soda
- ¼ tsp baking soda
- 1 tsp cinnamon
- 1 cup lemon slices

DIRECTIONS

1. In a bowl combine all wet ingredients
2. In another bowl combine all dry ingredients
3. Combine wet and dry ingredients together
4. Pour mixture into 8-12 prepared muffin cups, fill 2/3 of the cups
5. Bake for 18-20 minutes at 375 F
6. When ready remove from the oven and serve

BLUEBERRY MUFFINS

Serves: *8-12*
Prep Time: *10*   Minutes

Cook Time: *20*   Minutes

Total Time: *30*   Minutes

INGREDIENTS

- 2 eggs
- 1 tablespoon olive oil
- 1 cup milk
- 2 cups whole wheat flour
- 1 tsp baking soda
- ¼ tsp baking soda
- 1 tsp cinnamon
- 1 cup blueberries

DIRECTIONS

1. In a bowl combine all wet ingredients
2. In another bowl combine all dry ingredients
3. Combine wet and dry ingredients together
4. Fold in blueberries and mix well
5. Pour mixture into 8-12 prepared muffin cups, fill 2/3 of the cups
6. Bake for 18-20 minutes at 375 F, when ready remove and serve

KUMQUAT MUFFINS

Serves: *8-12*
Prep Time: *10*   Minutes

Cook Time: *20*   Minutes

Total Time: *30*   Minutes

INGREDIENTS

- 2 eggs
- 1 tablespoon olive oil
- 1 cup milk
- 2 cups whole wheat flour
- 1 tsp baking soda
- ¼ tsp baking soda
- 1 tsp cinnamon
- 1 cup kumquat

DIRECTIONS

1. In a bowl combine all wet ingredients
2. In another bowl combine all dry ingredients
3. Combine wet and dry ingredients together
4. Pour mixture into 8-12 prepared muffin cups, fill 2/3 of the cups
5. Bake for 18-20 minutes at 375 F
6. When ready remove from the oven and serve

CHOCOLATE MUFFINS

Serves: **8-12**

Prep Time: **10**   Minutes

Cook Time: **20**   Minutes

Total Time: **30**   Minutes

INGREDIENTS

- 2 eggs
- 1 tablespoon olive oil
- 1 cup milk
- 2 cups whole wheat flour
- 1 tsp baking soda
- ¼ tsp baking soda
- 1 tsp cinnamon
- 1 cup chocolate chips

DIRECTIONS

1. In a bowl combine all wet ingredients
2. In another bowl combine all dry ingredients
3. Combine wet and dry ingredients together
4. Fold in chocolate chips and mix well
5. Pour mixture into 8-12 prepared muffin cups, fill 2/3 of the cups
6. Bake for 18-20 minutes at 375 F

MUFFINS

Serves: **8-12**
Prep Time: **10**   Minutes

Cook Time: **20**   Minutes

Total Time: **30**   Minutes

INGREDIENTS

- 2 eggs
- 1 tablespoon olive oil
- 1 cup milk
- 2 cups whole wheat flour
- 1 tsp baking soda
- ¼ tsp baking soda
- 1 tsp cinnamon

DIRECTIONS

1. In a bowl combine all wet ingredients
2. In another bowl combine all dry ingredients
3. Combine wet and dry ingredients together
4. Pour mixture into 8-12 prepared muffin cups, fill 2/3 of the cups
5. Bake for 18-20 minutes at 375 F
6. When ready remove from the oven and serve

OMELETTE

Serves: *1*
Prep Time: *5*   Minutes

Cook Time: *10*   Minutes

Total Time: *15*   Minutes

INGREDIENTS

- 2 eggs
- ¼ tsp salt
- ¼ tsp black pepper
- 1 tablespoon olive oil
- ¼ cup cheese
- ¼ tsp basil

DIRECTIONS

1. In a bowl combine all ingredients together and mix well
2. In a skillet heat olive oil and pour the egg mixture
3. Cook for 1-2 minutes per side
4. When ready remove omelette from the skillet and serve

CARROT OMELETTE

Serves: *1*

Prep Time: 5   Minutes

Cook Time: *10*   Minutes

Total Time: *15*   Minutes

INGREDIENTS

- 2 eggs
- ¼ tsp salt
- ¼ tsp black pepper
- 1 tablespoon olive oil
- ¼ cup cheese
- ¼ tsp basil
- 1 cup carrot

DIRECTIONS

1. In a bowl combine all ingredients together and mix well
2. In a skillet heat olive oil and pour the egg mixture
3. Cook for 1-2 minutes per side
4. When ready remove omelette from the skillet and serve

ONION OMELETTE

Serves: *1*

Prep Time: *5* Minutes

Cook Time: *10* Minutes

Total Time: *15* Minutes

INGREDIENTS

- 2 eggs
- ¼ tsp salt
- ¼ tsp black pepper
- 1 tablespoon olive oil
- ¼ cup cheese
- ¼ tsp basil
- 1 cup red onion

DIRECTIONS

1. In a bowl combine all ingredients together and mix well
2. In a skillet heat olive oil and pour the egg mixture
3. Cook for 1-2 minutes per side
4. When ready remove omelette from the skillet and serve

BROCCOLI OMELETTE

Serves: **1**
Prep Time: **5** Minutes

Cook Time: **10** Minutes

Total Time: **15** Minutes

INGREDIENTS

- 2 eggs
- ¼ tsp salt
- ¼ tsp black pepper
- 1 tablespoon olive oil
- ¼ cup cheese
- ¼ tsp basil
- 1 cup broccoli

DIRECTIONS

1. In a bowl combine all ingredients together and mix well
2. In a skillet heat olive oil and pour the egg mixture
3. Cook for 1-2 minutes per side
4. When ready remove omelette from the skillet and serve

BEETS OMELETTE

Serves: *1*
Prep Time: 5 Minutes

Cook Time: *10* Minutes

Total Time: *15* Minutes

INGREDIENTS

- 2 eggs
- ¼ tsp salt
- ¼ tsp black pepper
- 1 tablespoon olive oil
- ¼ cup cheese
- ¼ tsp basil
- 1 cup beets

DIRECTIONS

1. In a bowl combine all ingredients together and mix well
2. In a skillet heat olive oil and pour the egg mixture
3. Cook for 1-2 minutes per side
4. When ready remove omelette from the skillet and serve

EGGPLANT ROLLATINI

Serves: **6-8**

Prep Time: **10** Minutes

Cook Time: **25** Minutes

Total Time: **35** Minutes

INGREDIENTS

- 1 eggplant
- 12 oz. ricotta cheese
- 2 oz. mozzarella cheese
- 1 can tomatoes
- ¼ tsp salt
- 2 tablespoons seasoning

DIRECTIONS

1. Lay the eggplant on a baking sheet
2. Roast at 350 F for 12-15 minutes
3. In a bowl combine mozzarella, seasoning, tomatoes, ricotta cheese and salt
4. Add cheese mixture to the eggplant and roll
5. Place the rolls into a baking dish and bake for another 10-12 minutes
6. When ready remove from the oven and serve

ASPARAGUS WITH EGG

Serves: **4-6**
Prep Time: **10**   Minutes

Cook Time: **25**   Minutes

Total Time: **35**   Minutes

INGREDIENTS

- 1 lb. asparagus
- 4-5 pieces prosciutto
- ¼ tsp salt
- 2 eggs

DIRECTIONS

1. Trim the asparagus and season with salt
2. Wrap each asparagus pieces with prosciutto
3. Place the wrapped asparagus in a baking dish
4. Bake at 375 F for 22-25 minutes
5. When ready remove from the oven and serve

DEVILED EGGS

Serves: *8*

Prep Time: *10* Minutes

Cook Time: *20* Minutes

Total Time: *30* Minutes

INGREDIENTS

- 8 eggs
- ½ cup Greek Yogurt
- 1 tablespoon mustard
- 1 tsp smoked paprika
- 1 tablespoon green onions

DIRECTIONS

1. In a saucepan add the eggs and bring to a boil
2. Cover and boil for 10-15 minutes
3. When ready slice the eggs in half and remove the yolks
4. In a bowl combine remaining ingredients and mix well
5. Spoon 1 tablespoon of the mixture into each egg
6. Garnish with green onions and serve

LEEK FRITATTA

Serves: **2**

Prep Time: **10**   Minutes

Cook Time: **20**   Minutes

Total Time: **30**   Minutes

INGREDIENTS

- ½ lb. leek
- 1 tablespoon olive oil
- ½ red onion
- ¼ tsp salt
- 2 ggs
- 2 oz. cheddar cheese
- 1 garlic clove
- ¼ tsp dill

DIRECTIONS

1. In a bowl whisk eggs with salt and cheese
2. In a frying pan heat olive oil and pour egg mixture
3. Add remaining ingredients and mix well
4. Serve when ready

KALE FRITATTA

Serves: **2**

Prep Time: **10**   Minutes

Cook Time: **20**   Minutes

Total Time: **30**   Minutes

INGREDIENTS

- 1 cup kale
- 1 tablespoon olive oil
- ½ red onion
- ¼ tsp salt
- 2 eggs
- 2 oz. cheddar cheese
- 1 garlic clove
- ¼ tsp dill

DIRECTIONS

1. In a skillet sauté kale until tender
2. In a bowl whisk eggs with salt and cheese
3. In a frying pan heat olive oil and pour egg mixture
4. Add remaining ingredients and mix well
5. Serve when ready

GREENS FRITATTA

Serves: **2**

Prep Time: **10** Minutes

Cook Time: **20** Minutes

Total Time: **30** Minutes

INGREDIENTS

- ½ lb. greens
- 1 tablespoon olive oil
- ½ red onion
- ¼ tsp salt
- 2 eggs
- 2 oz. parmesan cheese
- 1 garlic clove
- ¼ tsp dill

DIRECTIONS

1. In a bowl whisk eggs with salt and parmesan cheese
2. In a frying pan heat olive oil and pour egg mixture
3. Add remaining ingredients and mix well
4. Serve when ready

AVOCADO TOAST

Serves: **2**

Prep Time: **5**   Minutes

Cook Time: **5**   Minutes

Total Time: **10**   Minutes

INGREDIENTS

- 4 slices bread
- 1 avocado
- ¼ tsp red chili flakes
- ¼ tsp salt

DIRECTIONS

1. Toast the bread and set aside
2. Lay avocado slices on each bread slice
3. Sprinkle with red chili flakes and salt
4. Serve when ready

PUMPKIN FRENCH TOAST

Serves: **3**
Prep Time: **5**   Minutes

Cook Time: **15**   Minutes

Total Time: **20**   Minutes

INGREDIENTS

- ¼ cup milk
- 2 eggs
- ½ cup pumpkin puree
- 1 tablespoon pumpkin slice
- 6 bread slices

DIRECTIONS

1. In a bowl whisk all ingredients for the dipping
2. Dip the bread into the dipping and let it soak for 3-4 minutes
3. In a skillet heat olive oil and fry each slice for 2-3 minutes per side
4. When ready remove from the skillet and serve

COCONUT CHAI OATMEAL

Serves: **2**

Prep Time: **5**   Minutes

Cook Time: **15**   Minutes

Total Time: **20**   Minutes

INGREDIENTS

- ¼ cup oats
- ½ cup chia tea
- ¼ cup coconut milk
- 1 peach
- ¼ tsp coconut oil
- 1 tsp coconut flakes

DIRECTIONS

1. In a bowl combine together oats, coconut milk, chia tea and microwave until thickness
2. In a saucepan add peach slices and cook for 2-3 minutes
3. Place peaches over the oats and top with coconut flakes
4. Serve when ready

DESSERTS

BREAKFAST COOKIES

Serves: **8-12**

Prep Time: 5   Minutes

Cook Time: **15**   Minutes

Total Time: **20**   Minutes

INGREDIENTS

- 1 cup rolled oats
- ¼ cup applesauce
- ½ tsp vanilla extract
- 3 tablespoons chocolate chips
- 2 tablespoons dried fruits
- 1 tsp cinnamon

DIRECTIONS

1. Preheat the oven to 325 F
2. In a bowl combine all ingredients together and mix well
3. Scoop cookies using an ice cream scoop
4. Place cookies onto a prepared baking sheet
5. Place in the oven for 12-15 minutes or until the cookies are done
6. When ready remove from the oven and serve

BANANA BREAKFAST SMOOTHIE

Serves: **1**

Prep Time: **5**   Minutes

Cook Time: **5**   Minutes

Total Time: **10**   Minutes

INGREDIENTS

- ½ cup vanilla yogurt
- 2 tsp honey
- Pinch of cinnamon
- 1 banana
- 1 cup ice

DIRECTIONS

1. In a blender place all ingredients and blend until smooth
2. Pour the smoothie in a glass and serve

MANGO SMOOTHIE

Serves: **1**

Prep Time: **5** Minutes

Cook Time: **5** Minutes

Total Time: **10** Minutes

INGREDIENTS

- 1 cup coconut milk
- 1 cup vanilla yogurt
- 1 cup ice
- 1 banana
- 1 mango
- 1 tsp vanilla
- 1 tsp honey

DIRECTIONS

1. In a blender place all ingredients and blend until smooth
2. Pour smoothie in a glass and serve

POWER SMOOTHIE

Serves: *1*
Prep Time: 5   Minutes

Cook Time: 5   Minutes

Total Time: *10*   Minutes

INGREDIENTS

- 2 cups blueberries
- 1 cup pomegranate juice
- 1 cup ice
- 1 tablespoon chia seeds
- 1 banana

DIRECTIONS

1. In a blender place all ingredients and blend until smooth
2. Pour smoothie in a glass and serve

SPINACH SMOOTHIE

Serves: *1*

Prep Time: *5*   Minutes

Cook Time: *5*   Minutes

Total Time: *10* Minutes

INGREDIENTS

- 1 cup orange juice
- 1 cup coconut water
- 1 banana
- 1 mango
- 2 cups spinach

DIRECTIONS

1. In a blender place all ingredients and blend until smooth
2. Pour smoothie in a glass and serve

KALE DETOX SMOOTHIE

Serves: *1*
Prep Time: 5   Minutes
Cook Time: 5   Minutes
Total Time: *10*   Minutes

INGREDIENTS

- 1 banana
- 1 cup blueberries
- 1 tsp ginger
- 2 cups kale leaves
- 1 cup coconut water
- 1 pinch cinnamon

DIRECTIONS

1. In a blender place all ingredients and blend until smooth
2. Pour smoothie in a glass and serve

ENERGY BOOSTING SMOOTHIE

Serves: *1*
Prep Time: *5*   Minutes

Cook Time: *5*   Minutes

Total Time: *10*   Minutes

INGREDIENTS

- 1 banana
- 1 cup mango
- 1 cup blueberries
- 1 cup Greek Yogurt
- 1 tablespoon honey
- ¼ avocado

DIRECTIONS

1. In a blender place all ingredients and blend until smooth
2. Pour smoothie in a glass and serve

CRANBERRY SMOOTHIE

Serves: *1*

Prep Time: *5* Minutes

Cook Time: *5* Minutes

Total Time: *10* Minutes

INGREDIENTS

- ¼ cup oats
- 1 cup almond milk
- 1 cup cranberry juice
- ¼ cup orange juice
- 1 tablespoon honey
- 1 pinch cinnamon

DIRECTIONS

1. In a blender place all ingredients and blend until smooth
2. Pour smoothie in a glass and serve

MANDARIN SMOOTHIE

Serves: *1*

Prep Time: 5   Minutes

Cook Time: 5   Minutes

Total Time: *10*   Minutes

INGREDIENTS

- 1 cup coconut water
- 1 mandarin orange
- 1 cup frozen blueberries
- 1 tablespoon honey

DIRECTIONS

1. In a blender place all ingredients and blend until smooth
2. Pour smoothie in a glass and serve

PAPAYA SMOOTHIE

Serves: *1*

Prep Time: *5*   Minutes

Cook Time: *5*   Minutes

Total Time: *10*   Minutes

INGREDIENTS

- 1 banana
- ¼ cup yogurt
- 1 cup papaya
- 1 cup raspberries
- ¼ cup coconut milk
- 1 pinch cinnamon

DIRECTIONS

1. In a blender place all ingredients and blend until smooth
2. Pour smoothie in a glass and serve

PURPLE SMOOTHIE

Serves: **1**

Prep Time: **5**   Minutes

Cook Time: **5**   Minutes

Total Time: **10**   Minutes

INGREDIENTS

- 1 cup vanilla yogurt
- 1 cup blueberries
- 1 cup blackberries
- 1 cup strawberries
- 1 banana
- 2 tablespoons honey
- 1 cup ice

DIRECTIONS

1. In a blender place all ingredients and blend until smooth
2. Pour smoothie in a glass and serve

SECOND COOKBOOK

BREAKFAST

BEKEDD EGGS WITH VEGETABLE HASH

Serves: **2**

Prep Time: **10** Minutes

Cook Time: **20** Minutes

Total Time: **35** Minutes

INGREDIENTS

- ¼ cup tomatoes
- ½ cup zucchini
- ½ cup yellow pepper
- 1 tablespoon olive oil
- 1 avocado
- 2 eggs
- salt

DIRECTIONS

1. Preheat the oven to 400 F
2. In a casserole dish add vegetables and drizzle olive oil over vegetables, mix well
3. Cut avocado in half, crack the eggs into each avocado half and sprinkle salt

4. Bake avocado and vegetables for 18-20 minutes or until vegetables are soft and eggs started to thicken

5. When ready remove from the oven and serve

RUTABAGA HASH

Serves: **4**

Prep Time: **10** Minutes

Cook Time: **20** Minutes

Total Time: **30** Minutes

INGREDIENTS

- 2 tablespoons olive oil
- 1 rutabaga
- ¼ cup red onion
- ¼ cup red pepper
- 1 tsp salt
- ¼ tsp pepper
- ¼ tsp dill

DIRECTIONS

1. In a skillet heat olive oil and sauté rutabaga for 4-5 minutes
2. Cover and cook until rutabagas are tender
3. Add red pepper, onion, paprika and sauté for 8-10 minutes
4. Add dill, pepper, salt and combine
5. When ready remove to a plate

SAGE BREAKFAST PATTIES

Serves: **6**

Prep Time: **10** Minutes

Cook Time: **15** Minutes

Total Time: **25** Minutes

INGREDIENTS

- 1 lb. turkey
- 1 tablespoon sage
- 1 tablespoon onions
- ¼ tsp thyme
- ¼ tsp garlic flakes
- ¼ tsp salt
- 1 tablespoon olive oil

DIRECTIONS

1. In a bowl add all ingredients and mix well
2. Divide mixture into 4-6 portions and form 4-6 solid patties
3. In a skillet heat olive oil and cook each one for 4-5 minutes per side
4. When ready remove from skillet and serve

COCONUT CEREAL

Serves: **2**

Prep Time: **15** Minutes

Cook Time: **15** Minutes

Total Time: **30** Minutes

INGREDIENTS

- 1 cup almond flour
- ¼ tsp coconut
- 1 tsp cinnamon
- ¼ tsp salt
- ¼ tsp baking soda
- ¼ tsp vanilla extract
- 1 egg white
- 1 tablespoon olive oil

DIRECTIONS

1. Preheat the oven to 375 F
2. In a bowl combine baking soda, cinnamon, coconut, almond flour, salt and set aside
3. In another bowl combine vanilla extract, olive oil and mix well
4. In another bowl whisk the egg white and combine with vanilla extract mixture
5. Add almond flour to the vanilla extract mixture and mix well

6. Transfer dough onto a baking sheet and bake at 375 F for 10-15 minutes

7. When ready remove from the oven and serve

ZUCCHINI BREAD

Serves: *4*

Prep Time: *10* Minutes

Cook Time: *45* Minutes

Total Time: *55* Minutes

INGREDIENTS

- 1 zucchini
- 1 cup millet flour
- ½ cup almond flour
- ½ cup buckwheat flour
- 1 tsp baking powder
- ¼ tsp baking soda
- ¼ tsp salt
- ¼ cup almond milk
- 1 tsp apple cider vinegar
- 2 eggs
- ½ cup olive oil

DIRECTIONS

1. In a bowl combine almond flour, millet flour, buckwheat flour, baking soda, salt and mix well
2. In another bowl combine almond milk and apple cider vinegar
3. In a bowl beats eggs, add almond milk mixture and mix well

4. Add flour mixture to the almond mixture and mix well
5. Fold in zucchini and pour bread batter into pan
6. Bake at 375 F for 40-45 min
7. When ready remove from the oven and serve

BAKED EGGS WITH ONIONS

Serves: **2**

Prep Time: **10**   Minutes

Cook Time: **20**   Minutes

Total Time: **30**   Minutes

INGREDIENTS

- 1 tablespoon olive oil
- 1 red bell pepper
- 1 red onion
- 1 cup tomatoes
- ¼ tsp salt
- ¼ tsp pepper
- 2 eggs
- parsley

DIRECTIONS

1. In a saucepan heat olive oil and sauté peppers and onions until soft
2. Add salt, pepper, tomatoes and cook for 4-5 minutes
3. Remove mixture and form 2 patties
4. Break the eggs into each pattie, top with parsley and place under the broiler for 5-6 minutes
5. When ready remove and serve

Serves: **2**

Prep Time: **5**   Minutes

Cook Time: **5**   Minutes

Total Time: **10** Minutes

INGREDIENTS

- 1 cup coconut flakes
- ½ cup macadamia nuts
- 1 tablespoon chia seeds
- 1 tablespoon pumpkin seeds
- ¼ tsp cinnamon
- ¼ tsp ginger
- ¼ tsp nutmeg

DIRECTIONS

1. In a bowl combine all ingredients together
2. Place muesli in a container and refrigerate
3. When ready remove from the fridge and serve

MORNING SOUFFLE

Serves: **4**

Prep Time: **15**   Minutes

Cook Time: **35**   Minutes

Total Time: **50**   Minutes

INGREDIENTS

- ¼ cup green chilies
- 1 cup avocado
- 1 cup grilled chicken
- 2 onions
- 4 eggs
- ½ cup milk
- 1 tablespoon coconut flour
- 1 tsp salt
- ¼ tsp pepper

DIRECTIONS

1. Scatter green chillies in the bottom of a baking dish
2. Add chicken, onions, avocado over green chillies and set aside
3. In another bowl combine coconut flour with eggs, pepper, salt and pour egg mixture over vegetables
4. Bake at 350 F for 30-35 minutes
5. When ready garnish with cilantro and serve

BUCKWHEAT MUFFFNS

Serves: **8-12**
Prep Time: **10**   Minutes

Cook Time: **15**   Minutes

Total Time: **25**   Minutes

INGREDIENTS

- 1 cup buckwheat groats
- ½ cup coconut flakes
- ¼ cup walnuts
- ¼ cup pumpkin seeds
- 1 tablespoon chia seeds
- ¼ cup flaxseed meal
- 1 tsp cinnamon
- 2 eggs
- 1 cup almond milk
- ¼ cup almond butter
- 2 packets powdered stevia
- 1 tablespoon vanilla extract

DIRECTIONS

1. In a bowl soak buckwheat groats overnight
2. In a bowl combine pumpkin seeds, buckwheat groats, chia seeds, cinnamon, salt, walnuts, flaxseed meal and coconut flakes

3. In a bowl combine almond milk, powdered stevia, eggs and combine
4. Combine almond mix mixture with buckwheat mixture and pour mixture into 8-12 muffins cups
5. Bake at 350 F for 12-15 minutes
6. When ready remove from the oven and serve

MUSHROOM OMELETTE

Serves: *1*

Prep Time: *5*   Minutes

Cook Time: *10*   Minutes

Total Time: *15*   Minutes

INGREDIENTS

- 2 eggs
- ¼ tsp salt
- ¼ tsp black pepper
- 1 tablespoon olive oil
- ¼ cup cheese
- ¼ tsp basil
- 1 cup mushrooms

DIRECTIONS

1. In a bowl combine all ingredients together and mix well
2. In a skillet heat olive oil and pour the egg mixture
3. Cook for 1-2 minutes per side
4. When ready remove omelette from the skillet and serve

FRENCH TOAST

Serves: **4**

Prep Time: **10** Minutes

Cook Time: **20** Minutes

Total Time: **30** Minutes

INGREDIENTS

- 5 egg whites
- ½ cup low fat milk
- ¼ tsp cinnamon
- ½ tsp allspice
- 4 slices bread
- 1 tsp butter

DIRECTIONS

1. In a bowl mix egg whites, cinnamon, allspice and milk
2. Dip bread into batter and place in a skillet
3. Cook for 1-2 minutes per side or until golden
4. When ready, remove and serve

ORANGE MORNING COFFE

Serves: **2**

Prep Time: **5** Minutes

Cook Time: **5** Minutes

Total Time: **10** Minutes

INGREDIENTS

- ½ cup instant coffee
- ¾ cup sugar
- 1 cup Coffee Mate powder
- 1 tsp dried orange peel

DIRECTIONS

1. Place all ingredients in a blender and blend until powdered
2. Place 2 tsp of coffee mix in a cup
3. Add boiling water and mix, serve when ready

MORNING FRUIT COMPOTE

Serves: **1**
Prep Time: **10**   Minutes

Cook Time: **10**   Minutes

Total Time: **20**   Minutes

INGREDIENTS

- ½ cup strawberries
- ¼ cup blackberries
- ¼ cup peaches
- ½ cup raspberries
- ¼ cup orange juice
- 1 banana

DIRECTIONS

1. Pour orange juice into a container
2. Add remaining ingredients and toss well
3. Allow to rest overnight
4. Serve when ready

BAKED EGG CUSTARD

Serves: **4**

Prep Time: **10**   Minutes

Cook Time: **30**   Minutes

Total Time: **40**   Minutes

INGREDIENTS

- 2 eggs
- ½ cup low fat milk
- 2 tablespoons sugar
- 1 tsp vanilla
- 1 tsp nutmeg

DIRECTIONS

1. Preheat the oven to 300 F
2. In a bowl mix all ingredients using a hand mixer
3. Pour into muffin pans and sprinkle nutmeg
4. Bake for 25-30 minutes
5. When ready remove and serve

EGG OMELET

Serves:	*4*	
Prep Time:	*5*	minutes
Cook Time:	*10*	minutes
Total Time:	*15*	minutes

INGREDIENTS

- 3 eggs beaten
- 3 tablespoons 2% milk
- 2 teaspoons butter
- dash of pepper

DIRECTIONS

1. Beat eggs with milk and pepper
2. Heat butter in skillet and add eggs
3. When eggs are done roll one half over

GREEN CHILI CHEESE OMELETE

Serves:	*4*	
Prep Time:	*15*	minutes
Cook Time:	*0*	minutes
Total Time:	*15*	minutes

INGREDIENTS

- 1 tablespoon butter
- 4 eggs
- 4 tablespoons water
- 1 4-ounce can green chilies
- 4 oz. cheese

Sauce

- 1 tablespoon butter
- 1 tablespoon onion
- ¼ cup canned tomatoes

DIRECTIONS

1. Beat eggs and water together, meanwhile melt butter in skillet
2. Add egg mixture and reduce heat
3. Wrap chilies around each cheese strips
4. Serve on heated platter
5. For sauce melt butter and add tomato and onion

MACARONI AND CHEESE

Serves:	**4**
Prep Time:	**15** minutes
Cook Time:	**20** minutes
Total Time:	**35** minutes

INGREDIENTS

- 8 oz. macaroni
- 1 tablespoon canola oil
- 2 teaspoons chives
- ¾ teaspoon pepper
- 1 ½ cups natural cheese
- ½ cup 1,5% milk

DIRECTIONS

1. Heat 5-6 cups of water and add macaroni for about 8-10 minutes
2. Drain and rinse in cold water
3. Add canola oil and stir until macaroni is coated
4. Add milk, cheese, pepper and chives
5. Mix in cheese with macaroni and reduce heat
6. Continue cooking for 15-20 minutes
7. Add 1-2 tablespoons of milk

CREPES

Serves:	**6**	
Prep Time:	**10**	minutes
Cook Time:	**10**	minutes
Total Time:	**20**	minutes

INGREDIENTS

- 3 eggs
- 1 ¼ cups 1,5% milk
- ¾ cup sifted flour
- 1 tablespoon sugar
- ¼ teaspoon salt
- cooking spray

DIRECTIONS

1. Beat eggs until thick
2. Add salt and sugar
3. Add flour with milk beating with mixer
4. Spread batter evenly to make thin cakes
5. Turn when is brown

GRILLED CHEESE SANDWICH

Serves: **4**
Prep Time: **20**   minutes
Cook Time: **0**   minutes
Total Time: **20**   minutes

INGREDIENTS

- 2 tablespoons butter
- 8 slices bread
- 8 oz. Swiss cheese
- 1 4-ounce can green chills

DIRECTIONS

1. Spread butter on the side of four slices of bread
2. Place 1 ounce of Swiss cheese and one whole chili
3. Place cheese on split chili and top with remaining slice of bread
4. Heat skillet and place sandwiches in skillet
5. Grill on each side until cheese is melted

CINNAMON FRENCH TOAST

Serves:	*4*
Prep Time:	*5* minutes
Cook Time:	*10* minutes
Total Time:	*15* minutes

INGREDIENTS

- 2 eggs
- 1-2 tablespoons butter
- cinnamon
- ¾ cup light non-diary creamer
- 6 slices bread

DIRECTIONS

1. Combine eggs and creamer
2. Dup bread in egg mixture
3. Melt one tablespoon of butter
4. Sprinkle top side with cinnamon
5. If needed add more butter

PANCAKES

BANANA PANCAKES

Serves: **4**

Prep Time: **10** Minutes

Cook Time: **20** Minutes

Total Time: **30** Minutes

INGREDIENTS

- 1 cup whole wheat flour
- ¼ tsp baking soda
- ¼ tsp baking powder
- 1 cup mashed banana
- 2 eggs
- 1 cup milk

DIRECTIONS

1. In a bowl combine all ingredients together and mix well
2. In a skillet heat olive oil
3. Pour ¼ of the batter and cook each pancake for 1-2 minutes per side
4. When ready remove from heat and serve

AVOCADO PANCAKES

Serves: **4**

Prep Time: **5**   Minutes

Cook Time: **15**   Minutes

Total Time: **20**   Minutes

INGREDIENTS

- ¼ cup coconut flour
- ¼ tsp baking soda
- ¼ tsp salt
- 2 eggs
- ¼ cup almond milk
- ¼ avocado
- 2 green onions
- 1 tablespoon olive oil

DIRECTIONS

1. In a bowl combine dry ingredients with wet ingredients and mix well
2. In a skillet heat olive oil and pour ¼ batter and cook for 1-2 minutes per side
3. When ready remove to a place and serve with avocado slices

OLD FASHIONED PANCAKES

Serves: **4**

Prep Time: **10** Minutes

Cook Time: **20** Minutes

Total Time: **30** Minutes

INGREDIENTS

- 1 egg
- ½ cup sugar
- ½ tsp baking powder
- ½ cup low fat milk
- 1 tsp vegetable oil
- ½ cup all purpose flour

DIRECTIONS

1. In a bowl mix all purpose flour, egg, sugar, baking powder, milk and water
2. Pour ¼ cup batter in a skillet and cook for 1-2 minutes per side
3. When ready remove and serve

COOKIES

BREAKFAST COOKIES

Serves: **8-12**

Prep Time: **5** Minutes

Cook Time: **15** Minutes

Total Time: **20** Minutes

INGREDIENTS

- 1 cup rolled oats
- ¼ cup applesauce
- ½ tsp vanilla extract
- 3 tablespoons chocolate chips
- 2 tablespoons dried fruits
- 1 tsp cinnamon

DIRECTIONS

1. Preheat the oven to 325 F
2. In a bowl combine all ingredients together and mix well
3. Scoop cookies using an ice cream scoop
4. Place cookies onto a prepared baking sheet
5. Place in the oven for 12-15 minutes or until the cookies are done
6. When ready remove from the oven and serve

PINEAPPLE PUDDING

Serves: **4**

Prep Time: **10** Minutes

Cook Time: **20** Minutes

Total Time: **30** Minutes

INGREDIENTS

- 2 tablespoons all-purpose flour
- ½ cup sugar
- 1 egg
- 2 eggs
- 1 cup low fat milk
- 1 cup water
- 1 tsp vanilla extract
- 1 cup pineapple chunks
- ½ cup sugar
- 24-26 vanilla wafers

DIRECTIONS

1. Preheat the oven to 400 F
2. In a saucepan add sugar, egg, flour, egg yolks
3. Stir in water, milk and cook until water boils
4. Remove from heat, add vanilla extract and spread 1 tablespoon on the bottom of a casserole dish

5. Top with vanilla wafer and pineapples, continue with layers of custard, vanilla and wafers

6. Beat remaining egg whites using a hand mixer

7. Pile beaten egg whites on top of layered pudding

8. Bake for 8-10 minutes

9. Remove and serve

JEWELED COOKIES

Serves: *12*

Prep Time: *10*   Minutes

Cook Time: *15*   Minutes

Total Time: *25*   Minutes

INGREDIENTS

- 1 cup brown sugar
- 1 egg
- ½ cup milk
- ¼ cup unsalted butter
- 1 tsp vanilla
- 1 cup all-purpose flour
- 1 tsp baking powder
- 12 gumdrops

DIRECTIONS

1. Preheat the oven to 375 F
2. Cream butter, egg and sugar
3. Stir in vanilla and milk
4. In a bowl mix flour with baking powder and add remaining ingredients
5. Mix well and let it rest for 50-60 minutes
6. Drop dough onto cookie sheet

7. Bake for 10-12 minutes or until golden brown
8. Remove and serve

PUMPKIN SOUFFLE

Serves: *1*

Prep Time: *10* Minutes

Cook Time: *45* Minutes

Total Time: *55* Minutes

INGREDIENTS

- ¼ cup apple juice concentrate
- 1 can pumpkin
- 1 cup milk
- ¼ cup water
- ¼ tsp vanilla extract
- ¼ tsp ground nutmeg
- ¼ tsp all spice
- 1 tsp cinnamon
- ¼ cup grape nuts
- ¼ tsp pumpkin pie spice

DIRECTIONS

1. Preheat the oven to 375 F
2. In a bowl add all ingredients except grape nuts
3. In a pie plate add mixture and sprinkle grape nuts
4. Bake for 40-45 minutes, serve when ready

POUND CAKE

Serves: **4**

Prep Time: **10** Minutes

Cook Time: **30** Minutes

Total Time: **40** Minutes

INGREDIENTS

- ½ lb. butter
- ¾ cup sugar
- 3 eggs
- 1,5 cup bread flour
- 4 oz. milk

DIRECTIONS

1. Preheat the oven to 350 F
2. Cream butter and add sugar
3. Bell well, add flour, milk, eggs and mix
4. Pour batter in a baking dish and bake for 30 minutes
5. When ready remove and serve

SMOOTHIES

PUMPKIN SMOOTHIE

Serves: **1**

Prep Time: 5   Minutes

Cook Time: 5   Minutes

Total Time: **10**   Minutes

INGREDIENTS

- 2 tablespoons pumpkin
- 4 tablespoons coconut milk
- 1 tsp honey
- 1 banana
- ¼ tsp cinnamon
- 1 cup ice

DIRECTIONS

1. In a blender place all ingredients and blend until smooth
2. Pour smoothie in a glass and serve

KIWI SMOOTHIE

Serves: **1**

Prep Time: **5** Minutes

Cook Time: **5** Minutes

Total Time: **10** Minutes

INGREDIENTS

- 2 kiwis
- 2 bananas
- 1 cup soy milk
- 1 cup yogurt
- 2 tablespoons porridge oats
- 1 tsp honey

DIRECTIONS

1. In a blender place all ingredients and blend until smooth
2. Pour smoothie in a glass and serve

BERRY KALE SMOOTHIE

Serves: *1*

Prep Time: *5*   Minutes

Cook Time: *5*   Minutes

Total Time: *10*   Minutes

INGREDIENTS

- 1 handful kale
- 1 banana
- 1 cup berries
- 1 cup almond milk
- 1 cup protein powder

DIRECTIONS

1. In a blender place all ingredients and blend until smooth
2. Pour smoothie in a glass and serve

COCONUT SMOOTHIE

Serves: *1*
Prep Time: *5*   Minutes

Cook Time: *5*   Minutes

Total Time: *10* Minutes

INGREDIENTS

- 1 cup coconut milk
- ½ cup pineapple chunks
- 1 banana
- ½ cup pineapple juice
- 1 cup ice

DIRECTIONS

1. In a blender place all ingredients and blend until smooth
2. Pour smoothie in a glass and serve

AVOCADO SMOOTHIE

Serves: **1**

Prep Time: **5**   Minutes

Cook Time: **5**   Minutes

Total Time: **10**   Minutes

INGREDIENTS

- 1 cup coconut milk
- 1 cup pineapple chunks
- 1 avocado
- 1 banana
- 1 tsp vanilla extract
- 1 tablespoon hemp seeds
- 1 cup ice

DIRECTIONS

1. In a blender place all ingredients and blend until smooth
2. Pour smoothie in a glass and serve

TURMERIC SMOOTHIE

Serves: *1*

Prep Time: 5   Minutes

Cook Time: 5   Minutes

Total Time: *10*   Minutes

INGREDIENTS

- 1 banana
- 1 cup almond milk
- 1 tsp turmeric
- 1 tsp ginger
- 1 tsp cinnamon
- 1 tsp honey
- 1 cup ice

DIRECTIONS

1. In a blender place all ingredients and blend until smooth
2. Pour smoothie in a glass and serve

PAPAYA SMOOTHIE

Serves: *1*

Prep Time: 5   Minutes

Cook Time: 5   Minutes

Total Time: *10*   Minutes

INGREDIENTS

- 1 banana
- 1 cup papaya
- 1 cup blueberries
- 1 tsp cinnamon
- 1 cup spinach
- 1 tablespoon chia seeds
- 1 cup almond milk

DIRECTIONS

1. In a blender place all ingredients and blend until smooth
2. Pour smoothie in a glass and serve

APPLE SMOOTHIE

Serves: *1*
Prep Time: *5*   Minutes

Cook Time: *5*   Minutes

Total Time: *10*   Minutes

INGREDIENTS

- 1 apple
- 1 cup spinach
- 1 cup kale
- 1 cup ice

DIRECTIONS

1. In a blender place all ingredients and blend until smooth
2. Pour smoothie in a glass and serve

SIMPLE MUFFINS

Serves: *8-12*
Prep Time: *10*   Minutes
Cook Time: *20*   Minutes
Total Time: *30*   Minutes

INGREDIENTS

- 2 eggs
- 1 tablespoon olive oil
- 1 cup milk
- 2 cups whole wheat flour
- 1 tsp baking soda
- ¼ tsp baking soda
- 1 cup pumpkin puree
- 1 tsp cinnamon
- ¼ cup molasses

DIRECTIONS

1. In a bowl combine all wet ingredients
2. In another bowl combine all dry ingredients

3. Combine wet and dry ingredients together
4. Pour mixture into 8-12 prepared muffin cups, fill 2/3 of the cups
5. Bake for 18-20 minutes at 375 F
6. When ready remove from the oven and serve

Serves: *8*

Prep Time: *10* minutes

Cook Time: *25* minutes

Total Time: *35* minutes

INGREDIENTS

- ¾ cup boiling water
- ¾ cup cornmeal
- 2 eggs
- 1 tablespoon butter
- 1 tablespoon sugar
- ¼ teaspoon salt

DIRECTIONS

1. Heat oven at 375 degrees
2. Stir boiling water gradually into cornmeal
3. Beat egg whites until stiff and hold in reserve
4. Beat butter, yolks, egg, salt, sugar into cornmeal mixture
5. Bake for 25 minutes

OATMEAL RAISIN MUFFINS

Serves: **4**

Prep Time: **10** minutes

Cook Time: **15** minutes

Total Time: **25** minutes

INGREDIENTS

- 1 cup cake flour
- ½ cup white flour
- 2 teaspoons baking powder
- ¾ cup rolled oats
- ½ cup 1,5% milk
- 1 egg
- 4 tablespoons butter
- 3 tablespoons honey
- ½ cup raisins
- ½ cup water
- 1 ½ teaspoons cinnamon

DIRECTIONS

1. Sift the flour and baking powder
2. Mix in rolled oats and cinnamon
3. Beat egg, milk, butter and honey
4. Add raisins

5. Add the flour mixture and stir until ingredients are blended
6. Bake at 400 degrees for 10-12 minutes

BUTTER MUFFINS

Serves: **20**

Prep Time: **10**   Minutes

Cook Time: **30**   Minutes

Total Time: **40**   Minutes

INGREDIENTS

- 2 cups self-rising flour
- 6 oz. sour cream
- 1 cup unsalted butter

DIRECTIONS

1. Preheat the oven to 325 F
2. In a bowl stir together all ingredients
3. Spoon batter into muffins pans
4. Bake for 20-25 minutes or until browned
5. When ready, remove and serve

THIRD COOKBOOK

ZUCCHINI APPLE PANCAKES

Serves: **4**

Prep Time: **10**   minutes

Cook Time: **10**   minutes

Total Time: **20**   minutes

INGREDIENTS

- 1 zucchini
- 2 tablespoons almond butter
- 2 eggs
- 1 tablespoon honey
- 2 tablespoons coconut oil
- 1 apple
- 1 cup almond flour
- ¼ tsp baking powder
- ¼ tsp sea salt

DIRECTIONS

1. Mix zucchini, honey, apples, thyme and almond butter in a bowl
2. In another bowl mix salt, baking powder and flour and beat the eggs
3. Mix all the ingredients from the bowl and heat coconut oil in a fry pan

4. Pour the mixture in the pan and cook for 1-2 minutes each side

QUINOA AND GOJI BERRIES

Serves: **4**

Prep Time: **5**   Minutes

Cook Time: **10**   Minutes

Total Time: **15**   Minutes

INGREDIENTS

- 1 cup quinoa
- 1 cup goji
- parsley as needed

DIRECTIONS

1. Soak the quinoa and goji grains for 5-6 minutes in water
2. Cook quinoa until soft for 10-15 minutes
3. Roast the cumin seeds in a hot pan and stir in goji berries and sprinkle with parsley

Serves: **2**

Prep Time: **10**   Minutes

Cook Time: **20**   Minutes

Total Time: **30**   Minutes

INGREDIENTS

- 2 cloves garlic
- 2 sausages
- ¼ onion
- ¼ cup carrot
- 2 cups mushrooms
- 1 tsp coconut oil
- ¼ tablespoon parsley
- 2 cups asparagus

DIRECTIONS

1. Sauté the garlic and onions in coconut oil and add the rest of the ingredients
2. Add the sausages and cook for 5-10 minutes, serve when ready

GRAIN-FREE RICE

Serves: **3**

Prep Time: **10** Minutes

Cook Time: **10** Minutes

Total Time: **20** Minutes

INGREDIENTS

- 1 cauliflower heat
- 1 tablespoon salt
- 1 tablespoon pepper
- basil
- 1 tablespoon coconut oil
- 1 tablespoon parsley

DIRECTIONS

1. Grate the cauliflower to rice-grain
2. In a pan melt coconut oil add basil and add cauliflower and cook for 5-10 minutes
3. Cook until ready, remove and serve

HOMEMADE GRANOLA

Serves: **2**
Prep Time: **10** Minutes

Cook Time: **10** Minutes

Total Time: **20** Minutes

INGREDIENTS

- ¼ cup pumpkin seeds
- ¼ cup apricots
- 1 cup pecans
- ¼ cup almonds
- 1 cup coconut
- ½ cup coconut oil
- ½ cup honey
- 1 tsp cinnamon
- ¼ tsp nutmeg

DIRECTIONS

1. Preheat the oven to 325 F
2. Combine all the ingredients and toss well
3. Spread the mixture on a baking sheet (grease it with coconut oil) and bake for 10-15 minutes
4. When ready remove from oven and stir apricots
5. Let it cool and serve

CHIA SEED PUDDING

Serves: **2**

Prep Time: **10**   Minutes

Cook Time: **10**   Minutes

Total Time: **20**   Minutes

INGREDIENTS

- ¼ cup chia seeds
- 1 tsp honey
- 1 cup raspberries
- 1 cup coconut milk
- ¼ teaspoon vanilla essence
- 1 tsp salt

DIRECTIONS

1. Warm up milk and add salt
2. Add chia seeds and coconut oil in the milk and cook for 10-15 minutes
3. Whisk in the raspberries and mix
4. Serve when ready

MUSTARD CHICKEN SPREAD

Serves: **10**

Prep Time: **10** Minutes

Cook Time: **10** Minutes

Total Time: **20** Minutes

INGREDIENTS

- ¼ chicken
- 1 tablespoon tahini pate
- 1 tablespoon miso paste
- 1 tablespoon mustard
- 1 tablespoon olive oil
- 1 tablespoon truffle oil

DIRECTIONS

1. Mash the chicken and remove all the bones from it
2. Mix with miso, tahini paste and mustard
3. Combine all the ingredients and adjust the taste after your preference
4. Serve when ready

SAUSAGES WITH PICKLED CUCUMBERS

Serves: **2**
Prep Time: **10** Minutes

Cook Time: **10** Minutes

Total Time: **20** Minutes

INGREDIENTS

- 2 sausages
- ½ tsp olive oil
- 2 large picked cucumbers

DIRECTIONS

1. In a skillet add coconut oil and place the sausages
2. Cook the sausages each side for 4-5 minutes or until ready
3. Remove and serve with sliced pickles

SAUSAGE WITH ROASTED TOMATO

Serves: 2

Prep Time: **10**   Minutes

Cook Time: **30**   Minutes

Total Time: **40**   Minutes

INGREDIENTS

- 2 lamb sausages
- 2 tomatoes
- 2 tsp olive oil

DIRECTIONS

1. In a skillet add olive oil and add the sausages
2. Cut the tomatoes and place them in the skillet
3. Cook the sausages for 4-5 minutes each side
4. Remove when ready and serve

Serves: **4**

Prep Time: **10**   Minutes

Cook Time: **20**   Minutes

Total Time: **30**   Minutes

INGREDIENTS

- 1 onion
- 1 tsp cumin seeds
- 1 cup quinoa
- 1 cup water
- 1 roasted red pepper
- 1 cup mushrooms
- 1 tablespoon coconut oil
- 3 carrots
- 1 bunch of kale
- 1 squash

DIRECTIONS

1. Soak the quinoa grains for 5-6 minutes and cook for 10-15 minutes
2. In a pan fry add coconut oil and fry the onion, add mushrooms and carrots and cook for another 5-6 minutes
3. Add pepper and squash and continue cooking

4. In another pan roast cumin seeds and add to the mixture when the seeds are ready

5. Mix everything well and serve when ready

GREEN PLANTAIN PANCAKES

Serves: *2*

Prep Time: *10*   Minutes

Cook Time: *20*   Minutes

Total Time: *30*   Minutes

INGREDIENTS

- 2 green plantains
- 1 pinch salt
- 1 tsp coconut oil
- 2 tablespoons lime juice
- ½ cup coconut oil

DIRECTIONS

1. Mix the lime juice and plantain with salt and coconut oil in a blender
2. In a skillet add water and ghee
3. Spread the mixture in the skillet
4. Cook on low heat for 5-6 minutes each side
5. Remove and serve with savory filling

BASIL SMOOTHIE

Serves: **2**

Prep Time: **10**   Minutes

Cook Time: **20**   Minutes

Total Time: **30**   Minutes

INGREDIENTS

- 1 zucchini
- ½ cup olive oil
- 1 clove garlic
- ¼ tsp ground cumin
- ¼ cup water
- handful of basil
- 1 tablespoons parsley
- handful of sprouts
- ¼ cup carrot
- 1 tsp lime juice
- zest form ¼ lime
- ½ tsp salt

DIRECTIONS

1. In a blender place all the ingredients
2. Blend them and serve when ready

PUMPKIN SMOOTHIE

Serves: *1*

Prep Time: *10*   Minutes

Cook Time: *10*   Minutes

Total Time: *20*   Minutes

INGREDIENTS

- 1 cup lukewarm
- ¼ cup pumpkin puree
- ½ cup pecans
- 1 tablespoon flax seed
- dandelion leaves
- ½ fresh ginger root
- 1 tablespoon tahini
- 1 tablespoon coconut butter
- ½ teaspoon vanilla extract
- ½ teaspoon cinnamon
- ½ teaspoon camu camu
- pitch of salt

DIRECTIONS

1. Mix all the ingredients in a blender and serve when ready

AMARANTH PORRIDGE

Serves: **1**

Prep Time: **10**   Minutes

Cook Time: **30**   Minutes

Total Time: **40**   Minutes

INGREDIENTS

- 1 cup amaranth
- ¼ inch fresh ginger
- ¼ tsp salt
- ¼ apple cider vinegar
- 1 ¼ tsp turmeric
- 3 cups water
- 1tablespoon ghee
- ¼ tsp cumin
- ¼ tsp mustard seeds
- 1 tablespoon butter

DIRECTIONS

1. In a pan melt the ghee and add mustard seeds and cumin
2. Add water, salt and amaranth
3. Boil on low heat for 30 minutes
4. Remove from heat when ready and add turmeric

5. When ready serve with pumpkin seeds

EGGS AND SPINACH

Serves: *4*

Prep Time: *5*   Minutes

Cook Time: *10*   Minutes

Total Time: *15*   Minutes

INGREDIENTS

-    1 ½ tsp chilli flakes
-    4 eggs
-    3 ½ oz spinach
-    1 lb tomatoes

DIRECTIONS

1.   **Wilt the spinach**
2.   **Squeeze the excess water out**
3.   **Divide among 4 bowls**
4.   **Mix the tomatoes with the seasoning and chilli flakes**
5.   **Add to the spinach bowls**
6.   **Crack an egg into each bowl and bake for about 15 minutes in the preheated oven at 365F**

MORNING SAUSAGE

Serves: **4**

Prep Time: **15** Minutes

Cook Time: **35** Minutes

Total Time: **50** Minutes

INGREDIENTS

- 1 lb ground chicken
- 1 ½ tsp smoked paprika
- ½ tsp salt
- 1 ½ tsp rubbed sage
- 1/3 tsp white pepper
- 1/3 tsp thyme
- 1/5 tsp nutmeg
- 1 ½ tbs olive oil

DIRECTIONS

1. Mix the sage, ground meet, paprika, white pepper, nutmeg, thyme and salt
2. Form patties and place them on a baking sheet
3. Fry the patties in hot oil until brown on both sides
4. Serve immediately

BREAKFAST TACO

Serves: **2**

Prep Time: **10**   Minutes

Cook Time: **20**   Minutes

Total Time: **30**   Minutes

INGREDIENTS

- ¼ cup onion
- 1/3 cup green pepper
- 2 tsp sage
- Corn tortillas
- 1 lb turkey
- 1 tsp thyme
- 4 cups eggs
- 2 lb hash browns

DIRECTIONS

1. Mix hash browns and oil, then spread on a baking pan
2. Bake for about 20 minutes until browned
3. Scramble the eggs with onions and peppers
4. Combine the sage and thyme together
5. Fill a tortilla with ½ cup mixture, then microwave for about 15 seconds
6. Serve immediately

STUFFED POTATOES

Serves: **6**

Prep Time: **10**   Minutes

Cook Time: **20**   Minutes

Total Time: **30**   Minutes

INGREDIENTS

- 3 potatoes
- 1/3 cup scallions
- 3 eggs
- 1/3 tsp salt
- 3 tbs butter
- 1/3 tsp pepper
- ½ cup cheese
- ½ cup red pepper

DIRECTIONS

1. Prick potatoes with a fork and microwave for a few minutes until tender
2. Cut the potatoes lengthwise and scoop out the flesh
3. Cook the bell pepper, scallions and chopped potato flesh in melted butter for about 3 minutes
4. Add eggs, salt and pepper and cook 2 more minutes
5. Remove from heat and fold in the cheese

6. Stuff each potato half with the mixture, allow to cool and wrap with foil

7. Refrigerate overnight

8. Cook for about 10 minutes turning once

9. Serve immediately

AVOCADO TOAST

Serves: **2**

Prep Time: **5**   Minutes

Cook Time: **5**   Minutes

Total Time: **10** Minutes

INGREDIENTS
Pesto:
- 1 ½ tbs olive oil
- 1 tbs hot water
- 1/8 tsp black pepper
- ¼ tsp garlic powder
- 1/3 cup basil leaves
- ¼ cup walnuts
- 1 lemon

Toast:
- 1/3 tsp black pepper
- 2 tsp olive oil
- 4 slices bread
- 1 avocado

DIRECTIONS

1. Place the pesto ingredients into a food processor and pulse until smooth
2. Toast the bread

3. Divide the avocado slices

4. Spread pesto over avocado, then drizzle with lemon juice and olive oil

5. Serve immediately

MORNING BAKE

Serves: *12*
Prep Time: *10*   Minutes

Cook Time: *30*   Minutes

Total Time: *40*   Minutes

INGREDIENTS

- 4 eggs
- 3 cups hash brown
- 12 oz turkey sausage
- 1 bell pepper
- 1 cup cheese
- 2 cups milk
- 1 onion
- ½ tsp salt
- ¼ tsp black pepper

DIRECTIONS

1. Cook the onion, pepper and sausage until done
2. Stir together with frozen potatoes and ½ cup cheese, then place into a baking dish
3. Mix together milk, pepper, salt and eggs and pour over
4. Bake uncovered for about 30 minutes
5. Sprinkle with cheese and bake 2 more minutes

HAM OMELETTE

Serves: **2**

Prep Time: **10**   Minutes

Cook Time: **20**   Minutes

Total Time: **30**   Minutes

INGREDIENTS

- 4 eggs
- 1 tbs paprika
- 2 tbs olive oil
- ½ tbs onion powder
- ½ cup onion
- 1/3 cup ham
- ½ cup red pepper
- ½ tbs garlic powder

DIRECTIONS

1. Sauté the onion in hot oil
2. Add in the red pepper and sauté until roasted on edges
3. Add ham and paprika and cook 2 more minutes
4. Whisk together the eggs in a bowl
5. Scramble the eggs in hot oil in another skillet
6. Sprinkle with onion and garlic powder

7. Place the ham mixture on one half of the omelette and fold it
8. Serve immediately

QUICHE CUPS

Serves: *8*

Prep Time: *10*   Minutes

Cook Time: *30*   Minutes

Total Time: *40*   Minutes

INGREDIENTS

- 10 oz broccoli
- 2 drops hot sauce
- 1/3 tsp black pepper
- 4 eggs
- 1 cup cheese
- ½ cup bell peppers
- 1 green onion

DIRECTIONS

1. Squeeze the vegetables dry
2. Blend the ingredients together using a food processor
3. Divide among a lined muffin pan
4. Bake for about 30 minutes
5. Allow to cool, then serve

CHICKEN SAUSAGE

Serves: **4**

Prep Time: **5** Minutes

Cook Time: **10** Minutes

Total Time: **15** Minutes

INGREDIENTS

- ½ tsp red pepper flakes
- 1 ½ tsp maple syrup
- 3 tsp olive oil
- 1 ½ tsp sage
- 1 ½ tsp garlic powder
- 1 ½ tsp black pepper
- 1 lb. ground chicken

DIRECTIONS

1. Mix everything together except for the oil
2. Form patties from the mixture
3. Cook the patties in hot oil until cooked through
4. Serve immediately

BURRITO BOWL

Serves: **4**

Prep Time: **10**   Minutes

Cook Time: **15**   Minutes

Total Time: **25**   Minutes

INGREDIENTS

- 2 tbs olive oil
- ½ cup almond milk
- 2 tbs shallot
- 1 cup red pepper
- 1/3 cup salsa
- 2 eggs
- 2 egg whites
- ½ cup onion
- 2 avocados
- 15 oz pinto beans
- 2 tsp cumin
- 1 cup cherry tomatoes

DIRECTIONS

1. Sauté the onion until soft
2. Add the red peppers and cook until they are also soft

3. Add chili powder, pinto beans and cumin, cook a little more, then cover and turn the heat off

4. Chop the tomatoes and avocados

5. Combine ½ chopped avocado, shallot, salsa and almond milk in a food processor

6. Pulse until combined

7. Scramble the eggs and egg whites

8. Divide the bean mixture into bowls, top with avocado, tomatoes, eggs and drizzle with avocado sauce

9. Serve immediately

TART RECIPES

PEAR TART

Serves: *6-8*

Prep Time: 25   Minutes

Cook Time: 25   Minutes

Total Time: *50*   Minutes

INGREDIENTS

- 1 lb. pears
- 2 oz. brown sugar
- ½ lb. flaked almonds
- ¼ lb. porridge oat
- 2 oz. flour
- ¼ lb. almonds
- pastry sheets
- 2 tablespoons syrup

DIRECTIONS

1. Preheat oven to 400 F, unfold pastry sheets and place them on a baking sheet
2. Toss together all ingredients together and mix well
3. Spread mixture in a single layer on the pastry sheets
4. Before baking decorate with your desired fruits

5. Bake at 400 F for 22-25 minutes or until golden brown
6. When ready remove from the oven and serve

CARDAMOM TART

Serves: **6-8**

Prep Time: **25** Minutes

Cook Time: **25** Minutes

Total Time: **50** Minutes

INGREDIENTS

- 4-5 pears
- 2 tablespoons lemon juice
- pastry sheets

CARDAMOMO FILLING

- ½ lb. butter
- ½ lb. brown sugar
- ½ lb. almonds
- ¼ lb. flour
- 1 ¼ tsp cardamom
- 2 eggs

DIRECTIONS

1. Preheat oven to 400 F, unfold pastry sheets and place them on a baking sheet
2. Toss together all ingredients together and mix well
3. Spread mixture in a single layer on the pastry sheets
4. Before baking decorate with your desired fruits

5. Bake at 400 F for 22-25 minutes or until golden brown
6. When ready remove from the oven and serve

PIE RECIPES

PEACH PECAN PIE

Serves: **8-12**

Prep Time: **15**   Minutes
Cook Time: **35**   Minutes
Total Time: **50**   Minutes

INGREDIENTS

- 4-5 cups peaches
- 1 tablespoon preserves
- 1 cup sugar
- 4 small egg yolks
- ¼ cup flour
- 1 tsp vanilla extract

DIRECTIONS

1. Line a pie plate or pie form with pastry and cover the edges of the plate depending on your preference
2. In a bowl combine all pie ingredients together and mix well
3. Pour the mixture over the pastry
4. Bake at 400-425 F for 25-30 minutes or until golden brown
5. When ready remove from the oven and let it rest for 15 minutes

BUTTERFINGER PIE

Serves: *8-12*

Prep Time: *15*   Minutes

Cook Time: *35*   Minutes

Total Time: *50*   Minutes

INGREDIENTS

- pastry sheets
- 1 package cream cheese
- 1 tsp vanilla extract
- ¼ cup peanut butter
- 1 cup powdered sugar (to decorate)
- 2 cups Butterfinger candy bars
- 8 oz whipped topping

DIRECTIONS

1. Line a pie plate or pie form with pastry and cover the edges of the plate depending on your preference
2. In a bowl combine all pie ingredients together and mix well
3. Pour the mixture over the pastry
4. Bake at 400-425 F for 25-30 minutes or until golden brown
5. When ready remove from the oven and let it rest for 15 minutes

STRAWBERRY PIE

Serves: **8-12**

Prep Time: **15** Minutes

Cook Time: **35** Minutes

Total Time: **50** Minutes

INGREDIENTS

- pastry sheets
- 1,5 lb. strawberries
- 1 cup powdered sugar
- 2 tablespoons cornstarch
- 1 tablespoon lime juice
- 1 tsp vanilla extract
- 2 eggs
- 2 tablespoons butter

DIRECTIONS

1. Line a pie plate or pie form with pastry and cover the edges of the plate depending on your preference
2. In a bowl combine all pie ingredients together and mix well
3. Pour the mixture over the pastry
4. Bake at 400-425 F for 25-30 minutes or until golden brown
5. When ready remove from the oven and let it rest for 15 minutes

ACAI SMOOTHIE

Serves: **1**

Prep Time: 5   Minutes

Cook Time: 5   Minutes

Total Time: **10**   Minutes

INGREDIENTS

- 1 cup acai puree
- 1 banana
- 1 cup pomegranate juice
- 1 kiwi
- ½ lemon

DIRECTIONS

1. In a blender place all ingredients and blend until smooth
2. Pour smoothie in a glass and serve

BERRY SMOOTHIE

Serves: *1*

Prep Time: *5*   Minutes

Cook Time: *5*   Minutes

Total Time: *10*   Minutes

INGREDIENTS

- 1 cup strawberries
- 1 cup blueberries
- ½ cup orange juice
- ½ cup coconut water
- 1 cup ice

DIRECTIONS

1. In a blender place all ingredients and blend until smooth
2. Pour smoothie in a glass and serve

GREEN SMOOTHIE

Serves: **1**

Prep Time: **5** Minutes

Cook Time: **5** Minutes

Total Time: **10** Minutes

INGREDIENTS

- 2 stalks celery
- 4 cups spinach
- 1 pear
- 1 banana
- 1 tablespoon lime juice
- 1 cup coconut water
- 1 cup ice

DIRECTIONS

1. In a blender place all ingredients and blend until smooth
2. Pour smoothie in a glass and serve

SUNRISE SMOOTHIE

Serves: *1*

Prep Time: *5*   Minutes

Cook Time: *5*   Minutes

Total Time: *10*   Minutes

INGREDIENTS

- 2 cups kiwi
- 2 bananas
- 2 mangoes
- ½ cup pineapple
- 1 cup ice
- 1 cup coconut water
- 1 tablespoon honey

DIRECTIONS

1. **In a blender place all ingredients and blend until smooth**
2. **Pour smoothie in a glass and serve**

SOY SMOOTHIE

Serves: **1**

Prep Time: **5**   Minutes

Cook Time: **5**   Minutes

Total Time: **10**   Minutes

INGREDIENTS

- 2 cups blueberries
- 1 cup soy vanilla yogurt
- 1 cup soy milk
- 1 tsp vanilla essence

DIRECTIONS

1. In a blender place all ingredients and blend until smooth
2. Pour smoothie in a glass and serve

POWER SMOOTHIE

Serves: **1**

Prep Time: **5** Minutes

Cook Time: **5** Minutes

Total Time: **10** Minutes

INGREDIENTS

- 1 cup kale
- ¼ cup greens
- ¼ cup baby spinach
- ¼ cup greens
- ½ cup pineapple
- ½ cup blueberries
- 1 cup almon milk

DIRECTIONS

1. In a blender place all ingredients and blend until smooth
2. Pour smoothie in a glass and serve

OAT SMOOTHIE

Serves: *1*

Prep Time: 5   Minutes

Cook Time: 5   Minutes

Total Time: *10*   Minutes

INGREDIENTS

- 1 cup orange juice
- ¼ cup oats
- 1 tablespoon flaxseed meal
- 1 tablespoon honey
- 1 banana
- 1 cup ice

DIRECTIONS

1. In a blender place all ingredients and blend until smooth
2. Pour smoothie in a glass and serve

APPLE SMOOTHIE

Serves: *1*

Prep Time: *5*   Minutes

Cook Time: *5*   Minutes

Total Time: *10*   Minutes

INGREDIENTS

- 2 green apples
- 1 banana
- ½ cup almond milk
- 1 cup ice
- ¼ cup vanilla yogurt
- 1 tsp cinnamon
- ¼ tsp nutmeg

DIRECTIONS

1. In a blender place all ingredients and blend until smooth
2. Pour smoothie in a glass and serve

ICE-CREAM RECIPES

VANILLA ICE-CREAM

Serves: **6-8**

Prep Time: **15**   Minutes

Cook Time: **15**   Minutes

Total Time: **30**   Minutes

INGREDIENTS

- 1 cup milk
- 1 tablespoon cornstarch
- 1 oz. cream cheese
- 1 cup heavy cream
- 1 cup brown sugar
- 1 tablespoon corn syrup
- 1 vanilla bean

DIRECTIONS

1. In a saucepan whisk together all ingredients
2. Mix until bubbly
3. Strain into a bowl and cool
4. Whisk in favorite fruits and mix well
5. Cover and refrigerate for 2-3 hours

6. Pour mixture in the ice-cream maker and follow manufacturer instructions
7. Serve when ready

Serves: *6-8*

Prep Time: *15*   Minutes

Cook Time: *15*   Minutes

Total Time: *30*   Minutes

INGREDIENTS

- 4 egg yolks
- 1 cup black coffee
- 2 cups heavy cream
- 1 cup half-and-half
- 1 cup brown sugar
- 1 tsp vanilla extract

DIRECTIONS

1. In a saucepan whisk together all ingredients
2. Mix until bubbly
3. Strain into a bowl and cool
4. Whisk in favorite fruits and mix well
5. Cover and refrigerate for 2-3 hours
6. Pour mixture in the ice-cream maker and follow manufacturer instructions
7. Serve when ready

FOURTH COOKBOOK

GOAT'S CHEESE RAREBIT

Serves: **4**

Prep Time: **10** Minutes

Cook Time: **30** Minutes

Total Time: **40** Minutes

INGREDIENTS

- 1 oz. olive oil
- 150 ml soya milk
- 6 oz. goat cheese
- 1 oz. flour
- ½ tsp mustard
- pepper
- 1 egg yolk
- 4 bread slices

DIRECTIONS

1. In a saucepan add butter, cheese, soya milk and cook on low heat
2. Stir in flour and bring mixture to a boil
3. Remove from heat add mustard, pepper and whisk in the egg yolks
4. Toast the bread and spread mixture between the slices

5. Place on a grill and cook until golden

Serves: **2**

Prep Time: **10**   Minutes

Cook Time: **10**   Minutes

Total Time: **20**   Minutes

INGREDIENTS

- 7 oz. smoked mackerel fillets
- 2 onions
- 1 lemon
- 3 oz. cream cheese
- 1 tablespoon creamed horseradish
- pepper

DIRECTIONS

1. Cut mackerel into small chunks
2. In a bowl mix cream cheese, mackerel, creamed horseradish, onions and zest of 1 lemon
3. Mix with lemon juice and season with pepper and pate that should be ready

PESTO CREAM VEGGIE DIP

Serves: **4**

Prep Time: **10** Minutes

Cook Time: **30** Minutes

Total Time: **40** Minutes

INGREDIENTS

- 7 oz. basil pesto
- 3 oz. cream cheese
- 3 oz. sour cream
- 2 tablespoons parmesan cheese

DIRECTIONS

1. In a bowl add cream cheese, pesto, sour cream and parmesan cheese
2. Mix well and serve when ready

CAULIFLOWER CHEESE

Serves: **6**

Prep Time: **10** Minutes

Cook Time: **20** Minutes

Total Time: **30** Minutes

INGREDIENTS

- 1 cauliflower
- 500 ml milk
- 3 tablespoons flour
- 2 oz. butter
- 3 oz. cheddar cheese
- 2 tablespoons breadcrumbs

DIRECTIONS

1. Preheat the oven to 400 F
2. In a saucepan add cauliflower and cook for 5-8 minutes
3. Add milk, butter, flour and whisk until mixture boils
4. Stir in cheese and pour over the cauliflower
5. Scatter over the remaining cheese and breadcrumbs
6. Bake cauliflower cheese for 18-20 minutes

PUMPKIN RISOTTO

Serves: **4**

Prep Time: **10** Minutes

Cook Time: **30** Minutes

Total Time: **40** Minutes

INGREDIENTS

- 2 tablespoons olive oil
- 1 onion
- 500 ml chicken stock
- 10 sage leaves
- 6 oz. Arborio rice
- 9 oz. pumpkin
- 2 oz. butter
- 1 pinch black pepper
- parmesan cheese

DIRECTIONS

1. In a saucepan add ½ chicken stock and cook on low heat, add sage, onion, rice and continue to simmer
2. Add pumpkin, remaining stock and cook until stock is absorbed and pumpkin is soft
3. Stir in butter, season with pepper and divide into 2-3 servings
4. Add grated cheese and serve

MINCE WITH BASIL

Serves: **4**

Prep Time: **10** Minutes

Cook Time: **20** Minutes

Total Time: **30** Minutes

INGREDIENTS

- 1 lb. beef
- 1 garlic clove
- 1 chili
- 1 onion
- 1 oz. fresh basil
- 1 tablespoon soy sauce
- 1 tablespoon vegetable oil

DIRECTIONS

1. Fry garlic, chili and mince over medium heat
2. Add the rest of ingredients and cook for 18-20 minutes
3. Remove from heat and serve with rice

PORK CHOPS

Serves: *4*

Prep Time: *10* Minutes

Cook Time: *30* Minutes

Total Time: *40* Minutes

INGREDIENTS

- 2 pork chops
- 1 tsp mustard
- 1 tsp oil
- 1 spring onion
- 1 clove garlic
- 1 tablespoon breadcrumbs
- 1 pinch dried hers

DIRECTIONS

1. Preheat the oven to 375 F
2. Spread the mustard over the pork chop
3. In a bowl add garlic, dried herbs, breadcrumbs, onions and mix well
4. Spread the herb mixture on top of each pork chop
5. Bake for 20-25 minutes
6. Remove and serve with boiled potatoes

BEEF BURGERS

Serves: **4**

Prep Time: **10** Minutes

Cook Time: **20** Minutes

Total Time: **30** Minutes

INGREDIENTS

- 1 lb. minced beef
- 1 onion
- 1 pinch dried herb
- 1 pinch black pepper

DIRECTIONS

1. Preheat the grill to hot
2. In a bowl mix all ingredients together
3. Divide mixture into 4 portion and shape into patties
4. Grill for 5-6 minutes per side or until brown
5. Serve in a burger bun with potato fries

BAKED FISH

Serves: **4**

Prep Time: **10**   Minutes

Cook Time: **30**   Minutes

Total Time: **40**   Minutes

INGREDIENTS

- 1 lb. boneless fish fillets
- juice of 1 lemon
- 1 tablespoon unsalted butter
- 1 pinch rosemary

DIRECTIONS

1. Preheat the oven to 325 F
2. Place the fish in a shallow baking dish
3. In a bowl mix all remaining ingredients
4. Dot over fish fillets
5. Bake for 25 minutes or until fish is tender
6. Serve with vegetables

MINT COUSCOUS

Serves: **4**

Prep Time: **10** Minutes

Cook Time: **15** Minutes

Total Time: **25** Minutes

INGREDIENTS

- ½ lb. couscous
- 500 ml water
- 2 tablespoons mint
- 2 teaspoons olive oil

DIRECTIONS

1. In a saucepan bring water to a boil
2. Add couscous and cover with a lid
3. Drizzle oil, mint and cook until soft
4. Season with black pepper and serve with baked fish

TOMATO FRITATTA

Serves: **2**

Prep Time: **10** Minutes

Cook Time: **20** Minutes

Total Time: **30** Minutes

INGREDIENTS

- ½ lb. tomato
- 1 tablespoon olive oil
- ½ red onion
- ¼ tsp salt
- 2 eggs
- 2 oz. cheddar cheese
- 1 garlic clove
- ¼ tsp dill

DIRECTIONS

1. In a bowl whisk eggs with salt and cheese
2. In a frying pan heat olive oil and pour egg mixture
3. Add remaining ingredients and mix well
4. Serve when ready

YAM ROOT FRITATTA

Serves: **2**

Prep Time: **10** Minutes

Cook Time: **20** Minutes

Total Time: **30** Minutes

INGREDIENTS

- ½ cup yam root
- 1 tablespoon olive oil
- ½ red onion
- ¼ tsp salt
- 2 eggs
- 2 oz. cheddar cheese
- 1 garlic clove
- ¼ tsp dill

DIRECTIONS

1. In a bowl whisk eggs with salt and cheese
2. In a frying pan heat olive oil and pour egg mixture
3. Add remaining ingredients and mix well
4. Serve when ready

WATERCRESS FRITATTA

Serves: **2**

Prep Time: **10**   Minutes

Cook Time: **20**   Minutes

Total Time: **30**   Minutes

INGREDIENTS

- 1 cup watercress
- 1 tablespoon olive oil
- ½ red onion
- ¼ tsp salt
- 2 eggs
- 2 oz. cheddar cheese
- 1 garlic clove
- ¼ tsp dill

DIRECTIONS

1. In a bowl whisk eggs with salt and cheese
2. In a frying pan heat olive oil and pour egg mixture
3. Add remaining ingredients and mix well
4. Serve when ready

BROCCOLI FRITATTA

Serves: **2**

Prep Time: **10**   Minutes

Cook Time: **20**   Minutes

Total Time: **30**   Minutes

INGREDIENTS

- 1 cup broccoli
- 1 tablespoon olive oil
- ½ red onion
- ¼ tsp salt
- 2 eggs
- 2 oz. cheddar cheese
- 1 garlic clove
- ¼ tsp dill

DIRECTIONS

1. In a skillet sauté broccoli until tender
2. In a bowl whisk eggs with salt and cheese
3. In a frying pan heat olive oil and pour egg mixture
4. Add remaining ingredients and mix well
5. Serve when ready

MOZZARELLA STUFFED CHICKEN BREAST

Serves: **2**

Prep Time: **10**   Minutes

Cook Time: **25**   Minutes

Total Time: **35**   Minutes

INGREDIENTS

- 2 chicken breasts
- 1 tsp salt
- 6-7 asparagus spears
- ½ cup mozzarella cheese
- 2 tsp olive oil
- ½ cup bread crumbs

DIRECTIONS

1. Drizzle olive oil and salt over the chicken breast
2. Place the chicken breast in the breadcrumbs bowl and toss well
3. Cut the chicken breast and stuff mozzarella inside
4. Roast chicken breast with asparagus at 400 F for 20-25 minutes
5. When ready remove from the oven and serve

MACARONI AND CHEESE

Serves: **2**

Prep Time: **10** Minutes

Cook Time: **20** Minutes

Total Time: **30** Minutes

INGREDIENTS

- 1 cup macaroni
- 1 tablespoon olive oil
- 1 tablespoon all-purpose flour
- 1 tsp salt
- 1 tsp garlic powder
- 1 cup milk
- 1 cup mozzarella cheese
- ½ cup parmesan cheese

DIRECTIONS

1. In a skillet heat olive oil, stir in flour, garlic, salt, milk and cook on low heat
2. Add mozzarella, macaroni and mix well
3. When ready remove from heat and serve with parmesan cheese on top

BUTTERNUT SQUASH BISQUE

Serves: **4**

Prep Time: **10**   Minutes

Cook Time: **30**   Minutes

Total Time: **40**   Minutes

INGREDIENTS

- 1 tablespoon olive oil
- ¼ cup red onion
- ½ cup carrots
- 4 cups butternut squash
- 2 cups vegetable stock
- 1 tsp salt

DIRECTIONS

1. In a pot heat olive oil, add onion and cook until tender
2. Add squash and carrots to the pot
3. Add vegetable stock, salt and bring to a boil
4. Simmer on low heat until vegetables are tender
5. Blend the soup until smooth, return to the pot and cook for another 5-10 minutes
6. When ready remove from heat and serve

GARLIC CHICKEN

Serves: **2**

Prep Time: **10**   Minutes

Cook Time: **40**   Minutes

Total Time: **50**   Minutes

INGREDIENTS

- 2 tablespoons butter
- 1 tablespoon garlic powder
- 1 tsp rosemary
- 1 tsp salt
- 1 cup honey
- 4 chicken thighs

DIRECTIONS

1. In a saucepan melt butter, add garlic, rosemary, salt and simmer on low heat for 30-60 seconds
2. Add honey and dip the chicken into the mixture
3. Cook for 2-3 minutes, be sure to be well coated
4. Transfer to the oven and bake at 400 F for 30-35 minutes
5. When ready remove from the oven and serve

PASTA WITH CREAM SAUCE

Serves: *2*
Prep Time: *10*   Minutes

Cook Time: *30*   Minutes

Total Time: *40*   Minutes

INGREDIENTS

- 2 cups penne pasta
- 2 tablespoons butter
- 1 lb. chicken breast
- 1 tsp garlic
- 1 cup canned pumpkin
- ¼ cup heavy cream
- 1 tablespoon sage leaves
- ¼ tsp salt
- ¼ cup pecans

DIRECTIONS

1. Cook pasta and set aside
2. In a skillet melt butter, add garlic, chicken and cook on medium heat until chicken is cooked
3. Add pasta, pumpkin, heavy cream, sage, salt and pecans
4. Toss to coat and cook on low heat for 5-10 minutes
5. When ready remove from the pot and serve

ROASTED SQUASH

Serves: **3-4**
Prep Time: **10**   Minutes

Cook Time: **20**   Minutes

Total Time: **30**   Minutes

INGREDIENTS

- 2 delicata squashes
- 2 tablespoons olive oil
- 1 tsp curry powder
- 1 tsp salt

DIRECTIONS

1. Preheat the oven to 400 F
2. Cut everything in half lengthwise
3. Toss everything with olive oil and place onto a prepared baking sheet
4. Roast for 18-20 minutes at 400 F or until golden brown
5. When ready remove from the oven and serve

BRUSSELS SPROUT CHIPS

Serves: **2**
Prep Time: **10**   Minutes

Cook Time: **20**   Minutes

Total Time: **30**   Minutes

INGREDIENTS

- 1 lb. brussels sprouts
- 1 tablespoon olive oil
- 1 tablespoon parmesan cheese
- 1 tsp garlic powder
- 1 tsp seasoning

DIRECTIONS

1. Preheat the oven to 425 F
2. In a bowl toss everything with olive oil and seasoning
3. Spread everything onto a prepared baking sheet
4. Bake for 8-10 minutes or until crisp
5. When ready remove from the oven and serve

POTATO CHIPS

Serves: **2**

Prep Time: **10**   Minutes

Cook Time: **20**   Minutes

Total Time: **30**   Minutes

INGREDIENTS

- 1 lb. potatoes
- 1 tablespoon olive oil
- 1 tablespoon parmesan cheese
- 1 tsp garlic powder
- 1 tsp seasoning

DIRECTIONS

1. Preheat the oven to 425 F
2. In a bowl toss everything with olive oil and seasoning
3. Spread everything onto a prepared baking sheet
4. Bake for 8-10 minutes or until crisp
5. When ready remove from the oven and serve

CUCUMBER CHIPS

Serves: *2*
Prep Time: *10* Minutes

Cook Time: *20* Minutes

Total Time: *30* Minutes

INGREDIENTS

- 1 lb. cucumber
- 1 tablespoon olive oil
- 1 tablespoon parmesan cheese
- 1 tsp garlic powder
- 1 tsp seasoning

DIRECTIONS

1. Preheat the oven to 425 F
2. In a bowl toss everything with olive oil and seasoning
3. Spread everything onto a prepared baking sheet
4. Bake for 8-10 minutes or until crisp
5. When ready remove from the oven and serve

MINT PIZZA

Serves: **6-8**
Prep Time: **10**   Minutes

Cook Time: **15**   Minutes

Total Time: **25**   Minutes

INGREDIENTS

- 1 pizza crust
- 1 olive oil
- 1 garlic clove
- 1 cup mozzarella cheese
- 2 oz. mint
- 2 courgettes

DIRECTIONS

1. Spread tomato sauce on the pizza crust
2. Place all the toppings on the pizza crust
3. Bake the pizza at 425 F for 12-15 minutes
4. When ready remove pizza from the oven and serve

SAUSAGE PIZZA

Serves: *6-8*
Prep Time: *10* Minutes

Cook Time: *15* Minutes

Total Time: *25* Minutes

INGREDIENTS

- 2 pork sausages
- 1 tablespoon olive oil
- 2 garlic cloves
- 1 tsp fennel seeds
- ½ lb. ricotta
- 1 cup mozzarella cheese
- 1 oz. parmesan cheese
- 1 pizza crust

DIRECTIONS

1. Spread tomato sauce on the pizza crust
2. Place all the toppings on the pizza crust
3. Bake the pizza at 425 F for 12-15 minutes
4. When ready remove pizza from the oven and serve

HEALTY PIZZA

Serves: *6-8*
Prep Time: *10*   Minutes

Cook Time: *15*   Minutes

Total Time: *25*   Minutes

INGREDIENTS

- 1 pizza crust
- 1 tablespoon olive oil
- 1 garlic clove
- 1 cup tomatoes
- 1 cup mozzarella cheese
- 1 carrot
- 1 cucumber

DIRECTIONS

1. Spread tomato sauce on the pizza crust
2. Place all the toppings on the pizza crust
3. Bake the pizza at 425 F for 12-15 minutes
4. When ready remove pizza from the oven and serve

PASTA

SIMPLE SPAGHETTI

Serves: 2

Prep Time: 5   Minutes

Cook Time: 15   Minutes

Total Time: 20   Minutes

INGREDIENTS

- 10 oz. spaghetti
- 2 eggs
- ½ cup parmesan cheese
- 1 tsp black pepper
- Olive oil
- 1 tsp parsley
- 2 cloves garlic

DIRECTIONS

1. In a pot boil spaghetti (or any other type of pasta), drain and set aside
2. In a bowl whish eggs with parmesan cheese
3. In a skillet heat olive oil, add garlic and cook for 1-2 minutes
4. Pour egg mixture and mix well
5. Add pasta and stir well

6. When ready garnish with parsley and serve

CORN PASTA

Serves: 2

Prep Time: 5   Minutes

Cook Time: 15   Minutes

Total Time: 20   Minutes

INGREDIENTS

- 1 lb. pasta
- 4 oz. cheese
- ¼ sour cream
- 1 onion
- 2 cloves garlic
- 1 tsp cumin
- 2 cups corn kernels
- 1 tsp chili powder
- 1 tablespoon cilantro

DIRECTIONS

1. In a pot boil spaghetti (or any other type of pasta), drain and set aside
2. Place all the ingredients for the sauce in a pot and bring to a simmer
3. Add pasta and mix well
4. When ready garnish with parmesan cheese and serve

ARTICHOKE PASTA

Serves: **2**

Prep Time: **5**   Minutes

Cook Time: **15**   Minutes

Total Time: **20**   Minutes

INGREDIENTS

- ¼ cup olive oil
- 1 jar artichokes
- 2 cloves garlic
- 1 tablespoon thyme leaves
- 1 lb. pasta
- 2 tablespoons butter
- 1. Cup basil
- ½ cup parmesan cheese

DIRECTIONS

1. In a pot boil spaghetti (or any other type of pasta), drain and set aside
2. Place all the ingredients for the sauce in a pot and bring to a simmer
3. Add pasta and mix well
4. When ready garnish with parmesan cheese and serve

CHICKEN PASTA

Serves: **2**

Prep Time: **5**   Minutes

Cook Time: **15**   Minutes

Total Time: **20**   Minutes

INGREDIENTS

- 1 lb. cooked chicken breast
- 8 oz. pasta
- 2 tablespoons butter
- 1 tablespoon garlic
- 1 tablespoon flour
- ½ cup milk
- ½ cup heavy cream
- 1 jar red bell peppers
- 2 tablespoons basil

DIRECTIONS

1. In a pot boil spaghetti (or any other type of pasta), drain and set aside
2. Place all the ingredients for the sauce in a pot and bring to a simmer
3. Add pasta and mix well
4. When ready garnish with parmesan cheese and serve

SALAD

CARROT AND ORANGE WITH GINGER SALAD

Serves: **1**

Prep Time: **5**   Minutes

Cook Time: **5**   Minutes

Total Time: **10** Minutes

INGREDIENTS

- 16 oz carrots
- 2 oranges
- 2 tbs dill
- 1 tsp ginger

DIRECTIONS

1. Over a bowl, peel off and cut the white pith and outer membrane from one orange
2. Grate 1 tsp of the peel and squeeze the juice from the second orange in a bowl and add the ginger and chopped carrots
3. Add the peeled orange and dill and mix well

BROCCOLI AND RICE SALAD

Serves: 2

Prep Time: 5   Minutes

Cook Time: 15   Minutes

Total Time: 20   Minutes

INGREDIENTS

- 1 cup rice
- 1 cup broccoli
- 1 cup paneer
- 2 tbsp oil
- a pinch pepper
- 1 tsp lemon juice
- a pinch of ground ginger

DIRECTIONS

1. Boil the rice and chop the broccoli
2. Mix all the ingredients and serve

RICE AND FENNEL SALAD

Serves: 2

Prep Time: 5   Minutes

Cook Time: 30   Minutes

Total Time: 35   Minutes

INGREDIENTS

- 1 cup rice
- 2 fennel bulbs
- 1 celery stalk
- 1 red pepper
- 2 tbsp oil
- 2 tbsp lemon juice
- 2 tbsp mint
- 2 tbsp parsley
- a pinch salt
- a pinch pepper

DIRECTIONS

1. Put rice in a bowl and pour water and soak in for 25-30 minutes
2. Drain the rice and then steam with chopped pepper and set aside
3. Combine all ingredients in a bowl and serve

Serves: *4*
Prep Time: *10* Minutes

Cook Time: *30* Minutes

Total Time: *40* Minutes

INGREDIENTS

- 2 cups yogurt
- a pinch salt
- a pinch pepper
- 2 tbsp chopped mint
- 2 cucumbers

DIRECTIONS

1. Peel the cucumber and chop it
2. Combiner all the ingredients and serve

GREEN SALAD

Serves: **2**

Prep Time: **5** Minutes

Cook Time: **5** Minutes

Total Time: **10** Minutes

INGREDIENTS

- 4 leaves kale
- 1 romaine heart
- 1 cup parsley leaves
- 1 cup cilantro leaves
- ¼ fennel bulb
- 1 carrot
- salad dressing

DIRECTIONS

1. In a bowl mix all ingredients and mix well
2. Serve with dressing

CANDIDA GREEN SALAD

Serves: 2

Prep Time: 5   Minutes

Cook Time: 5   Minutes

Total Time: 10   Minutes

INGREDIENTS

- ½ avocado
- 2 bolied eggs
- 2 tablespoons olive oil
- 2 tablespoons apple cider vinegar
- Oregano
- 1 cup spinach leaves
- 1 cucumber
- ½ cup asparagus
- ½ cup broccoli stems
- ½ avocado

DIRECTIONS

1. In a bowl mix all ingredients and mix well
2. Serve with dressing

KALE & MIXED GREENS SALAD

Serves: **2**

Prep Time: **5**   Minutes

Cook Time: **5**   Minutes

Total Time: **10**   Minutes

INGREDIENTS

- 1 bunch kale
- 1 tablespoon olive oil
- 1 cup baby salad greens
- 1 carrot
- 1 small beet
- 1 celery stalk
- ¼ red bell pepper
- ¼ cup herbs
- ¼ steamed broccoli

DIRECTIONS

1. In a bowl mix all ingredients and mix well
2. Serve with dressing

QUINOA SALAD

Serves: **2**

Prep Time: **5** Minutes

Cook Time: **5** Minutes

Total Time: **10** Minutes

INGREDIENTS

- 1 cooked chicken breast
- ¼ cup cooked quinoa
- 1 cup spinach
- 1 tomato
- ¼ cucumber
- 1 avocado
- 1 shallot
- 1 garlic clove
- 1 tablespoon olive oil

DIRECTIONS

1. In a bowl mix all ingredients and mix well
2. Serve with dressing

BRUSSELS SPROUT SALAD

Serves: **2**

Prep Time: **5**   Minutes

Cook Time: **5**   Minutes

Total Time: **10**   Minutes

INGREDIENTS

- 1 tablespoon olive oil
- 1 cup shallots
- ½ cup celery
- 1 clove garlic
- 6-8 brussels sprouts
- 1 tablespoon thyme leaves
- Herbs

DIRECTIONS

1. In a bowl mix all ingredients and mix well
2. Serve with dressing

CHINESE SALAD

Serves: **2**

Prep Time: **5**   Minutes

Cook Time: **5**   Minutes

Total Time: **10**   Minutes

INGREDIENTS

- 1 head cabbage
- 1 cup carrot
- ¼ cup scallions
- ¼ cup radishes
- ½ cup mint
- 1 cup cooked chicken breast

DIRECTIONS

1. In a bowl mix all ingredients and mix well
2. Serve with dressing

BASIL & AVOCADO SALAD

Serves: **2**

Prep Time: **5**   Minutes

Cook Time: **5**   Minutes

Total Time: **10**   Minutes

INGREDIENTS

- **1 cup cooked chicken breast**
- **¼ cup basil leaves**
- **1 avocado**
- **1 tablespoon olive oil**
- **¼ tsp black pepper**

DIRECTIONS

1. **In a bowl mix all ingredients and mix well**
2. **Serve with dressing**

Serves: 2

Prep Time: 5   Minutes

Cook Time: 5   Minutes

Total Time: 10   Minutes

INGREDIENTS

- 1 roasted chicken
- ¼ cup olive oil
- ¼ cup cilantro
- 1 red onion
- 1 head romaine lettuce
- ¼ lemon
- 1 cucumber
- 1 tomato

DIRECTIONS

1. In a bowl mix all ingredients and mix well
2. Serve with dressing

THANK YOU FOR READING THIS BOOK!

CPSIA information can be obtained
at www.ICGtesting.com
Printed in the USA
LVHW031755010421
683230LV00001B/8